Copyright © Ecaabooks
Copyright © text and design: Jacquelyn Nicholson
Copyright © Art Work: Jacquelyn Nicholson
Copyright © Photography: Jacquelyn Nicholson
https://www.instagram.com/ecaabooks/
https://www.facebook.com/Ecaabooks/
https://twitter.com/Ecaabooks

All rights reserved. Without limiting the rights above, no part of this publication may be reproduced or transmitted, in any form or by any means (electronic, mechanical, photocopying, recording or otherwise) without the prior written permission of both the copyright owner and the above publisher of this book.

The photographs and art work in this book have been included to enhance the readers overall experience. Any relationship between the photographs and the subject matter is purely coincidental.

© 2022 by the author of this book. The book author retains sole copyright to his or her contributions to this book

The Blurb-provided layout designs and graphic elements are copyright Blurb Inc., © 2022. This book was created using the Blurb creative publishing service. The book author retains sole copyright to his or her contributions to this book.

Fun Facts
of
Christmas

2nd. Edition

Intro

The main reason for Christmas is the birth of Jesus Christ, But long ago, it wasn't always celebrated on the 25th of December. It didn't become an official holiday until the third century. But there are many other fun, interesting facts that most people don't know about Christmas. In fact, the Bible talks about Jesus being born around the harvest celebrations, which is why he was born in a manger or barn. Because all the accommodation in the area at the time was booked out. They were full of people celebrating the end of the harvest season.

As a young child, I was always told that the AD in the years represented after the death of Jesus, as most people just assumed that's what it meant. Whereas it actually meant after his birth. It comes from the Latin words' of Anno Domini, meaning: 'In the year of our Lord and BC represents Before Christ was born. Or before Jesus.

Christmas has become a commercialized season, but many aspects of this valued holiday are still linked to the past. Traditions from around the world were created over time by people worshiping and honoring this son of God called Jesus Christ.

In this book, we will look at some of the traditions of Christmas and where they came from. Some may be similar or slightly different in different parts of the world. See how many are your favorite ones.

Jingle Bells was first written for Thanks Giving, not for Christmas, and was composed by James Pierpont in Massachusetts, America, in 1850.

Emperor Constantine, a Roman Christian, declared that the 25th of December was the day to celebrate the birth of Jesus Christ, and the first recorded Christmas was held in 336 AD.

The Advent Calendar is a unique calendar that helps people count down to Christmas eve and the 12 days of Christmas that follows from the 25th of December to the 5th of January.

The tradition of hanging stockings on the fireplace comes from...

A poor man had three daughters for whom he could not afford to provide a dowry for each of them. St. Nicholas found out and went to help the man secretly. He dropped three bags of gold, one for each daughter. Over three nights, he went in through the man's window, and the gold bags fell into the drying stockings. The daughters then had dowries and could get married, avoiding being sold off into slavery.

Brenda Lee was 13 years old when she first recorded "Rockin' Around the Christmas Tree" in 1958. The song has since gone on to be recorded by hundreds of artists, making it one of the most successful Christmas songs of all time.

Father Christmas, Saint Nicholas, and Santa Claus are all associated with gift-giving to children during the Christmas season. These figures are closely related to each other and are often interchangeable.

In America, the first Christmas was held in 1539, when the people gathered to celebrate the season, minus any trees or giving of gifts.

Christmas is celebrated to represent the spirit of giving, which is why so many gifts are exchanged.

The author Washington Irving is best known for writing his books The Legend of sleepy hollow and Headless Horseman. He wrote many books about St Nicholas, and in 1819 he imagined Santa Claus with eight tiny rain deers.

Washington Irving loved Santa Claus so much that he helped create the Saint Nicholas Society in 1835 in the City of New York and served as secretary until 1841.

Gifts are shared during Christmas to symbolize the gifts given to Jesus Christ by the three wise men.

1640 – Scotland abolished the observance of Christmas (until 1958, when it became a legal holiday).

1377 – During a Christmas feast hosted by King Richard the II of England in 1377, three hundred sheep and twenty-eight oxen were consumed.

In the 12th century, French nuns would leave socks filled with tangerines, nuts, and other fruits at the houses of the poor.

Santa Claus delivering presents comes from Hollands' celebration of Saint Nicholas feast day, which is held on the 6th of December. Children would leave shoes out the night before and, in the morning, would find little gifts that St. Nicholas would leave them.

The 12 days of Christmas are from the 25th of December to the 5th of January. These are the holy days spent celebrating Jesus' birth; over time, man has crumbed everything into just one day on the 25th.

Many people find it very hard to believe that Jesus Christ is the Son of God, but they find it very easy to believe Hercules is the son of another god.

The giant iconic spruce tree that sits in Trafalgar Square each year has been gifted to the people of London from the Norwegian people ever since 1947 in gratitude for the British support during World War II, bringing goodwill towards all men yearly.

The original lyrics to "Hark! The Herald Angel Sings" was "Hark! How the Welkin rings!" Welkin is an old English term for Heaven. However, a preacher later tweaked the lyric.

Over time, many live trees dry out and catch fire, causing hundreds of house fires with an average of 10 deaths yearly because people forget to water their live Christmas trees.

The "Candle" represents Jesus as a Divine Light that every Christian should follow, the same light that led the Three Wise Men.

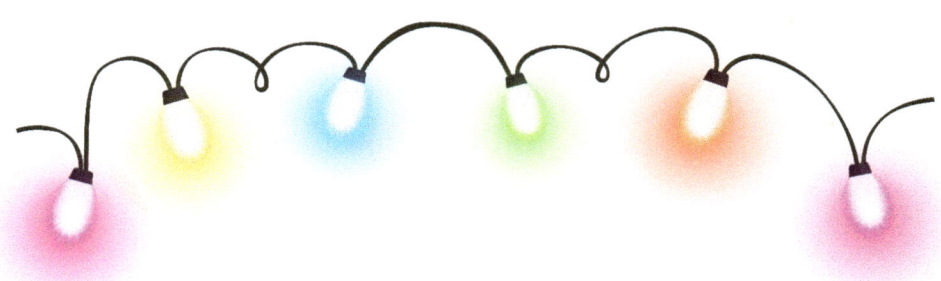

Santa Claus comes from St. Nicholas, a Christian bishop living in Turkey in the fourth century AD. St. Nicholas inherited a great deal of wealth and was known for giving it away to help the needy. When he became a saint, he became the protector of children.

The Advent and Christmas wreaths are constructed of evergreens to represent everlasting life brought through Jesus Christ. The wreath's circular shape represents God, with no beginning and no end. Christmas wreaths are also connected with the pagan holiday of Yule, marking the winter solstice, which was celebrated by ancient Germanic and Scandinavian peoples.

Boston, Massachusetts, receives a tree from Nova Scotia, Canada, because of the support given to the city of Halifax in 1917 when they experienced an explosion and fire disaster.

In 1915 Hallmark introduced their first Christmas cards.

Rio de Janeiro, Brazil, has the largest floating Christmas tree in the world; it is 278 feet tall.

Each year, approximately ten million Christmas turkeys are eaten in the UK and 22 million in the United States.

In 1836 Alabama was the first US state to set Christmas as a legal holiday, and in 1907 Oklahoma was the last.

1962 – the United States issued the first Christmas postage stamp.

It takes, on average, 6-8 years for a Christmas tree to be fully grown, but it can take as long as fifteen years.

The song "Santa Claus Is Coming to Town" has a genuinely depressing back-story. The songwriter, James Haven Gillespie, was broke and jobless, and his brother had just died when he was asked to write a Christmas song. He was initially overcome with grief but eventually found inspiration in his brother's death and their Christmas memories.

Boston church leaders tried to ban the song "I Saw Mommy Kissing Santa Claus" in the 1950s because they thought it promoted physical intimacy. So singer Jimmy Boyd had to fly to Boston and explain to them why it wasn't obscene.

After his death, the legend of St. Nicholas spread. St. Nick's name became Sint-Nicolaas in Dutch or Sinter Klaas for short. Which soon became known as Santa Claus.

\

"The Partridge" in a pear tree is Jesus Christ. So both "my true love" and "the partridge in a pear tree" represent Jesus — the partridge because it's a bird that will sacrifice its life to save its children.

Two Turtle Doves - are the Old and New Testaments of the Bible.

Three French Hens - stand for Faith, Hope, and Love.

The Four Calling Birds - are the four gospels of Matthew, Mark, Luke, and John.

The five golden rings - recalled the Torah or law, the first five books of the Old Testament.

The Six Geese a-laying - stands for the six days of the creation.

Seven Swans a-swimming - represent the sevenfold gifts of the Holy Spirit - Prophesy, Serving, Teaching, Exhortation, Contribution, Leadership, and Mercy.

The Eight Maids a-milking - are the eight beatitudes.

The Nine Ladies dancing is the nine fruits of the Holy Spirit - Love, Joy, Peace, Patience, Kindness, Goodness, Faithfulness, Gentleness, and Self Control.

The Ten Lords a-leaping - are the Ten Commandments.

The Eleven Pipers Piping - stands for the eleven faithful disciples.

The Twelve Drummers drumming - Symbolizes the twelve points of belief in the Apostle's Creed.

CHRIST-MAS is because we can't have Christmas without CHRIST!

The Christmas star symbolizes the star of Bethlehem, which according to the Biblical story, guided the kings or wise men to the baby Jesus. The star is also the heavenly sign of a prophecy fulfilled long ago and the shining hope for humanity.

During 1659 - 1681 celebrating Christmas was outlawed. Anyone caught celebrating this festive day was faced with fines. This is because the day was so unimportant after the revolutionary War.
The new Congress held its first session on the 25th of December in 1789. It took another century before Christmas was proclaimed a federal holiday.

Construction workers placed the first Rockefeller Christmas tree at the center of the site. Although it was a small undecorated tree in 1931, another tree had lights two years later.

Candy Canes became popular in 1847 when German and Swedish immigrants started hanging candy canes on a Christmas trees. Originally candy canes were used to keep children quiet during extended church services.

Fun Facts of Christmas

During World War II, the United States Playing Card Company joined forces with the American and British Intelligence Agencies to create an extraordinary playing deck of cards. They were given out as Christmas gifts to help allied prisoners of war to escape from German P.O.W. camps. The individual cards would peel apart when moistened to reveal maps with escape routes.

In 1931 Coca-Cola hired Haddon Sundblom to make Santa look more friendly in illustration.

The color red is used at Christmas to represent the blood of Jesus when he died on the cross. It's also reflected in the color of holly berries, which also had pagan symbolism during the winter solstice celebrations in ancient Rome. Green signifies everlasting light and life, and gold represents Jesus, the Son of God, royalty.

The candy cane treat represents the shape of a shepherd's crook. Jesus, often called the Good Shepherd, was born on Christmas. His birth was God's way to bring lost lambs back to the fold. The red stripe represents the blood of Christ's sacrifice, and the white represents his purity.

The wreath is a symbol of the eternal love of Jesus toward mankind. Holly also stands for immortality, and cedar for strength. Today, the wreath symbolizes generosity, giving, and family gatherings. For example, hanging a wreath on the front door for Christians, allowing Jesus to enter.

Bells are rung during Christmas to proclaim the season's arrival and to announce the birth of Jesus. The ringing of bells can also be traced back to pagan winter celebrations used to drive out evil spirits.

The word Christmas originates from the words Christ's Mass. In old English (first recorded in 1038), it was referred to as Cristesmæsse, which literally means 'Christian Mass.'

The word Noel entered the English language in the late 1300s. It originated from the Latin word Natalis which means the day of birth.

The best-selling Christmas song ever is White Christmas by Bing Crosby. It has sold more than 50 million copies around the world.

Christmas lights were invented in 1882 by Edward Johnson.

There are approximately 60 million trees grown in Europe each year.

Christmas is one of the most profitable times of year for many businesses.

Mistletoe is a parasitic plant, which means it lives on the tree it is attached to; without it, the mistletoe would die. The plant has long been a symbol of love, and some believe that the Druids used mistletoe as a cure-all, or some stories claim that it could promote fertility.

The spider web is a tradition due to the Eastern European tale of the Christmas spider, which led to the reason for tinsel at Christmas time.

The modern-day version of the story is that a woman immaculately cleaned her house for Christmas. The house spiders were swept to the farthest reaches. The spiders learned a beautiful Christmas tree was in the room and wanted a closer look. They saw the tree and loved it so much that they danced all over it. The spiders left their webs behind. Then Father Christmas, Jesus or Santa Claus saw the beautiful webs and miraculously transformed them into silver and gold tinsel so the woman who worked hard to clean her house would not be dismayed. In honor of that tale, people hang tinsel on their Christmas trees, and it has become a custom to include a spider among the decorations.

The world's biggest snowman was 113 feet tall and was built in Maine.

The white color during Christmas is a vivid representation of peace and purity! During winter, the snow that is witnessed in places around the world is also white. On various occasions, white wafers are used to decorate the Christmas tree. These wafers represent the bread eaten during Christian Communion, a time people remembered because of when Jesus died on the cross. In addition, in most churches, white is used as the color of Christmas.

The paradise tree or Christmas tree is about Adam and Eve.

Christmas Eve is the feast day of our first parents, Adam and Eve, commemorated as Saints in the calendars of the Catholic churches of Eastern rites.

Earlier, red represented the apples laden on the Paradise tree. The red apple color represented the fall of Adam. Red is also considered the color of the Holly berries, meaning the blood of Jesus Christ, who died on the cross. Also, the Bishop's robe's color was red and was first worn by St. Nicholas, which then became the uniform of Santa.

More than 160 countries around the world celebrate Christmas.

The eight days before Christmas in Italy, also known as the Novena, are filled with carolers singing traditional songs around the neighborhood.

The 8th of December is when many Italian homes and towns first put out their decorations, while a cannon is fired from Rome's Castel Sant'Angelo to mark the start of the celebrations. The season continues until Epiphany on the 6th of January, when the Three Wise Men arrived in Bethlehem.

The Giant Lantern Festival (Ligligan Parul Sampernandu) is held each year on the Saturday before Christmas Eve in San Fernando – the Christmas Capital of the Philippines." The festival attracts spectators from all over the country and across the globe. Eleven barangays (villages) participate in the festival, and competition is fierce as everyone pitches in, trying to build the most elaborate lantern. Initially, the lanterns were simple creations around half a meter in diameter, made from 'papel de hapon' (Japanese origami paper) and lit by candle.

Since 1966, a 13-meter-tall Yule Goat has been built in the center of Gävle's Castle Square each year for The Advent in Sweden for Christmas.

In Germany Weihnachtsmann (Father Christmas), Nikolaus travels by donkey in the middle of the night on the 6th of December (Nikolaus Tag) and leaves little treats like coins, chocolate, oranges, and toys in the shoes of good children all over Germany. In the Bavarian region. St. Nicholas also visits children in schools or at home, and in exchange for sweets or a small present, each child must recite a poem, sing a song or draw a picture.

"The Little Candles Day" (Día de las Velitas) marks the start of the Christmas season across Colombia. In honor of the Virgin Mary and the Immaculate Conception, people place candles and paper lanterns in their windows, balconies, and front yards. The tradition of candles has grown, and now entire towns and cities across the country are lit up with great displays.

In Venezuela, Every Christmas Eve, the city residents head to church in the early morning. But, for reasons known only to them, they do so on roller skates. This unique tradition is so popular that roads across the city are closed to cars so that people can skate to church safely before heading home for the traditional Christmas dinner of 'tamales' (a wrap made out of cornmeal dough and stuffed with meat, then steamed).

These countries don't celebrate Christmas. They include Afghanistan, Algeria, Azerbaijan, Bahrain, Bhutan, Cambodia, Iran, Israel, Japan, Kuwait, Laos, Libya, Maldives, Mauritania, North Korea, Oman, Pakistan, Saudi Arabia, Somalia, Tajikistan, Thailand, Turkmenistan, United Arab Emirates, Uzbekistan, Vietnam, and Yemen.

Angels, to most people, symbolize love, peace, and joy. Christmas angels can be everywhere, from appearing on Christmas cards and ornaments to being seen as figurines or within nativity scenes.

The Gift Bow symbolizes Christian commitment, bound to everlasting goodwill.

According to the Christian Bible's New Testament, Melchior, Balthazar, and Gaspar brought gifts of gold, incense, and myrrh to the newborn baby Jesus.

A candle flame is a mirror of starlight and also a symbol representing the star of Bethlehem. Before electric Christmas tree lights were invented, families would use candles to light up the tree. Also, during this season, two other holidays share the significance of candles and light: Hanukkah, the Festival of Lights in Judaism, and Kwanzaa, a unity celebration of people displaced during the African diaspora, where one candle of the kinara candle holder is lit over seven nights.

Every year in America, nearly 15000 people visit hospital emergency wards during November and December due to Christmas-related accidents.

Christmas is sometimes known as Noel or Xmas.

In Toronto, the annual Cavalcade of Lights marks the official start of the holiday season. The first Cavalcade took place in 1967 to show off Toronto's newly constructed City Hall and Nathan Phillips Square. The Square and Christmas tree are illuminated by more than 300,000 energy-efficient LED lights that shine from dusk until 11 pm until the New Year. On top of that, there are spectacular fireworks shows and outdoor ice skating.

Every Christmas Eve, the North American Aerospace Defense Command (NORAD) adjusts its satellites to track Santa on his journey worldwide. The favorite holiday tradition started in the 1950s when a young child accidentally called a NORAD command center looking for jolly old Saint Nick.

Fun Facts of Christmas

Blue is a significant color of the Christmas season which represents the mother of Jesus. In earlier times, blue dye color was more expensive than that of gold. Only the people from the royal families and kings used to wear blue because they were important people in the whole community. Mary was painted blue during Christmas to show that she was a significant community person.

The Christmas tree origins go back to the Egyptians and Romans, who marked the winter solstice with the evergreens as a reminder that spring would return soon. But it was Prince Albert of Germany who presented a Christmas Tree to his wife, Queen Victoria of England, and soon afterward, the tradition took off.

Fun Facts of Christmas

The first tinsel was invented in 1610 in Germany, made out of pure silver. However, in the United States, the government banned this tinsel because of the continence of lead, which could contribute to lead poisoning.

The first batch of eggnog in America had been created at the settlement that Captain John Smith helped start, Jamestown, in 1607, and the name eggnog comes from the word grog meaning any drink made with rum.

Christmas Eve traditions can be found in Norway, where people hide their brooms. It's a tradition that dates back centuries to when people believed witches and evil spirits came out on Christmas Eve looking for brooms to ride on. To this day, many people still hide their brooms in the safest place in the house to stop them from being stolen.

The Jewish holiday of Hanukkah is celebrated with much fanfare across the United States, with one of the most elaborate events taking place on a national stage. Since 1979, a giant nine-meter Menorah has been raised on the White House grounds for the eight days and nights of Hanukkah.

Fun Facts of Christmas

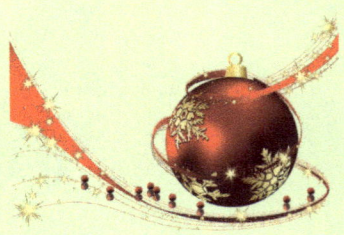

Author's Special Links

Follow my page on instagram - find out what I'm up to next and what new books are being released or just follow what I am doing and enjoy the photos I post.

https://www.instagram.com/jacquelyn_nicholsonauthor/

My books are available at Book Depository
https://www.bookdepository.com/author/Jacquelyn-Nicholson

or direct from my website
https://www.ecaabooks.au/

Fun Facts of Christmas

Homemade Play-dough

- 1 cup of oil
- 6 cups flour
- 250ml (1 cup) water

Play-dough is cheap and easy to make, and once you've made it, your child will enjoy playing with it for hours. This recipe makes an all-white play dough. No need to add messy food coloring!

Mix ingredients together in a large bowl, adding a little water at a time.

Knead well until the mixture is soft, smooth, and supple.

Squish away!

Equipment: Large bowl and wooden spoon

Keep it in an air-tight container, so it doesn't dry when your child has finished playing with it.

Fun Facts of Christmas

Index

Copyright	2
Title page	3
Intro	4
Fun Facts	6 - 35
Play-Dough	37
Author's Special Links	39
Index	41
Authors Other Books	42
Christmas Pictures	46

Author's Other books

Santa's Happy Holidays, Aussie Style
Softcover: ISBN: 9780368162787
Hardcover, ImageWrap: ISBN: 9780368162794
https://au.blurb.com/b/9253684-santa-s-happy-holidays-aussie-style

A Humble Poetry Book
Softcover: ISBN: 9781364822514
Hardcover, Dust Jacket: ISBN: 9781364822507
Hardcover, ImageWrap: ISBN: 9781364822521
https://au.blurb.com/b/6593017-a-humble-poetry-book

165 Ways to Make Your Heart Fly
Softcover ISBN: 9781714175802
Hardcover, Dust Jacket ISBN: 9781714175819
Hardcover, ImageWrap ISBN: 9781714175826
https://www.blurb.com/b/9685728-165-ways-to-make-your-heart-fly

Life Changes
Softcover: ISBN: 9780368871672
PDF: https://au.blurb.com/b/9498625-life-changes

Genealogy Made Easy
https://au.blurb.com/ebooks/605105-genealogy-made-easy
Softcover: ISBN: 9781366710710
Hardcover, Dust Jacket: ISBN: 9781366710703
Hardcover, ImageWrap: ISBN: 9781366710727
PDF: https://au.blurb.com/b/7566791-genealogy-made-easy

Psychology of Thinking 1
A Collective of Poems
Softcover: ISBN: 9781364874094
Hardcover, Dust Jacket: ISBN: 9781364874070
Hardcover, ImageWrap: ISBN: 9781364874087
PDF: https://au.blurb.com/b/6564432-psychology-of-thinking-1

Love Hurts
Softcover ISBN: 9780464591269
Hardcover, Dust Jacket ISBN: 9780464591276
Hardcover, ImageWrap ISBN: 9780464591283
https://www.blurb.com/b/9775274-love-hurts

Tasmania's Cradle

https://au.blurb.com/ebooks/541334-tasmania-s-cradle

Softcover: ISBN: 9781320488358

Hardcover, ImageWrap: ISBN: 9781320488365

PDF: https://au.blurb.com/b/6394771-tasmania-s-cradle

South Australia - In Picture Form Vol 1

Softcover: ISBN: 9781366254474

Hardcover, ImageWrap: ISBN: 9781366254481

PDF: https://au.blurb.com/b/7800155-south-australia

Santa Brings on Christmas

Softcover ISBN: 9780464525301

Hardcover, ImageWrap ISBN: 9780464525295

PDF: https://www.blurb.com/b/9749157-santa-brings-on-christmas

Provoking the Senses

Softcover ISBN: 9780464621935

Hardcover, Dust Jacket ISBN: 9780464621959

Hardcover, ImageWrap ISBN: 9780464621942

https://www.blurb.com/b/9789708-provoking-the-senses

Walk the Narrow Path to Righteousness
Softcover: ISBN: 9781366874528
Hardcover, Dust Jacket: ISBN: 9781366874535
Hardcover, ImageWrap: ISBN: 9781366874511
PDF: https://au.blurb.com/b/7462178-walk-the-narrow-path-to-righteousness

Shark Attack
Softcover: ISBN: 9780368407543
Hardcover, ImageWrap: ISBN: 9780368407536
PDF: https://au.blurb.com/b/9344014-shark-attack

Lightning and Thunderstorms
True Stories
Soft-cover ISBN: 9798210550781
Hardcover, Dust Jacket ISBN: 9798210550798
Hardcover, ImageWrap ISBN: 9798210550774

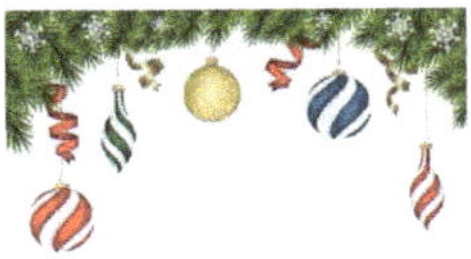

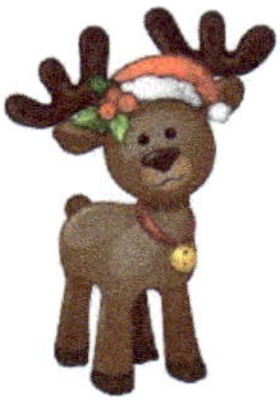

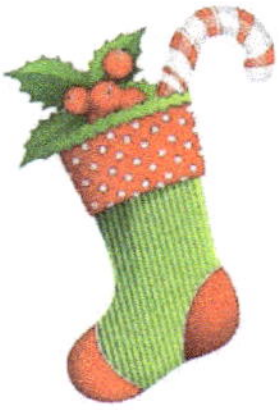

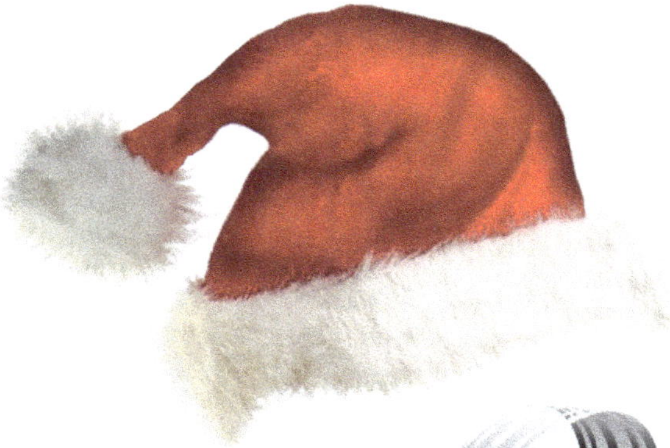

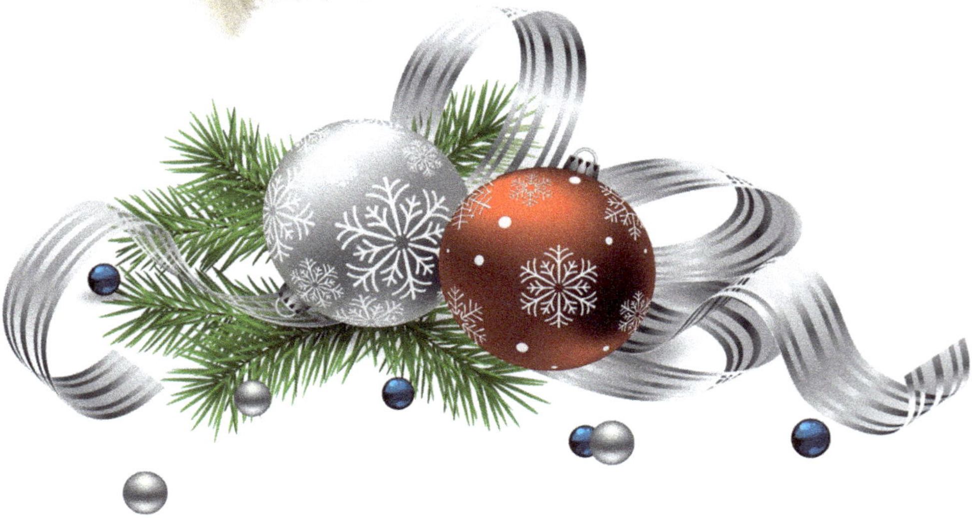

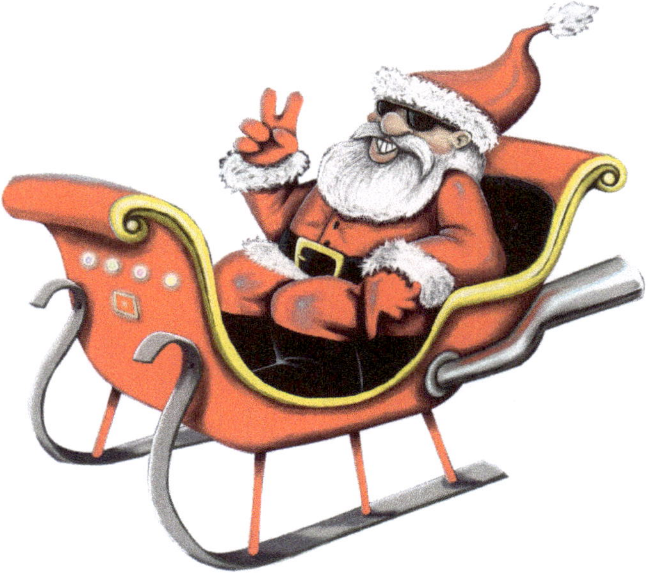

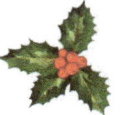